MONSTERS AND GROTESQUES
in Medieval Manuscripts

Ceste beste senefie le deable.

Ceste beste uaint les sainz et hypocrite la oreut.

MONSTERS AND GROTESQUES
in Medieval Manuscripts

ALIXE BOVEY

UNIVERSITY OF TORONTO PRESS

ICI EST SEORS ELIANGELS KI ENFERME LES PORTES

MONSTERS AND GROTESQUES
in Medieval Manuscripts

A monster is a thing deformed against kind, both of man or of beast or of anything else, and that is clept a monster.

Sir John Mandeville, Travels, chapter 7

A tiny one-footed beast, not much taller than one of the letters in the script above its head, lies on its back and uses its giant foot as an umbrella (1). This creature, called a sciopod, hopped its way from classical antiquity to the end of the Middle Ages, through travellers' tales of faraway lands and books of beasts, to find its way onto a page of the prayer book made for a wealthy bishop in about 1302. Medieval art is teeming with monsters who made similar journeys from antique mythology, literature and art; others came from scripture, the writings of medieval authors, and the prolific imaginations of medieval artists. These monsters inhabit corners and column capitals, peer down from ceiling bosses in cathedrals, slither around small ivories, and squat under the seats in choir stalls. Nowhere are they more abundant than in illuminated

1. A sciopod in the Breviary of Renaud de Bar, Bishop of Metz. France, c.1302. Yates Thompson MS 8, f.250v.

manuscripts, which collectively preserve more medieval art than any other type of object. Dragons decorate margins, twist into letter forms, and squeeze into the spaces at the end of lines of text (2, 3). Commonplace animals are fused in impossible combinations; human bodies merge with animal forms in ways that are often both comic and grotesque. For medieval people, these humorous and hideous creatures were a tantalizing suggestion of unknown worlds and unthinkable dangers, at once entertaining and electrifying, funny and frightening.

According to the *Oxford English Dictionary*, monsters are extraordinary or unnatural creatures, abnormal or deviant in physique or behaviour, often of unusual

2. Monsters, birds, and a knife-wielding man make up the letter 'A' in a canon law book. England (Christ Church, Canterbury), c.1120–1130. Cotton MS Claudius E V, f.25v.

proportions and, in some cases, exceptionally wicked. The monstrous creatures considered in this book appear in images painted or drawn on the pages of medieval manuscripts. Some resemble animals and humans, others are demonic; many combine the physical features of different creatures to create monsters that are simultaneously familiar and alien. Many of these creatures are fantastical products of artistic invention, produced in order to entertain, and probably nobody has seriously believed in their existence. But not all medieval monsters can be dismissed simply as flights of fantasy. Some monsters were based on real animals that people might have seen or heard about, such as snakes, whales and lions. Other types of monsters were symbolic expressions of ideas in which medieval Christians believed devoutly, whether or not they believed that monsters existed in the physical world. The majority of medieval people most certainly believed in the demons and devils who lurk in the margins of manuscripts. These metaphysical monsters represented spiritual dangers, while others surely expressed the manifold physical dangers that threatened life in the Middle Ages. Forests, wildernesses and foreign lands were dangerous places, and the medieval imagination filled them with monsters.

In the pages that follow, we shall explore the pantheon of medieval monsters in images from manuscripts in the British Library, seeking their roots in antiquity, the Bible, and the imaginations of artists, authors, and scribes.

The spread of Christianity across Europe during the first millennium A.D. gradually displaced the ancient pagan religions of Europe. The new religion did not, however, sweep away all vestiges of ancient civilization: rather, Christianity proved adept at absorbing and adapting aspects of pagan culture which did not conflict with Christian beliefs. The monsters of antique myth and history were among the cultural survivals that found new life in the hands of Christian writers and artists.

Reports of monstrous creatures and humanoid races that inhabited distant regions reached the Middle Ages from many ancient sources. Deformed creatures, many with human features, were said to inhabit faraway lands such as Ethiopia and India. Ancient Greek writers, including Aristotle, Homer, and Herodotus, described monstrous creatures and men living in Africa and the Indian subcontinent. Herodotus, writing c.450 B.C., mentions mountain-dwelling people with feet like goats, and one-eyed peoples who battled griffins, while Ctesias, a Greek physician writing about fifty years later, provided a richly detailed description of the wondrous creatures inhabiting India. During the Middle Ages, one the most influential of these writers was the Roman historian Pliny the Elder (23–79 A.D.), whose *Natural History* was one of the most important sources of information about the monstrous races during the Middle Ages. Pliny, whose accounts of the monstrous races that inhabited foreign lands were indebted to earlier Greek writers, was in turn abridged by Solinus, writing in the third century A.D.

3. Biting monsters decorate initials and borders in a Psalter. England (Oxford?), c.1265–1270
Add. MS 50,000, f.232v.

4. *A blemmyae, as described in the* Wonders of the East. *England (Winchester?), c.1025–1050. Cotton MS Tiberius B V, f.82r.*

Stories of the monstrous races written about by Ctesias, Pliny and Solinus were reshaped late in the tenth century in an Anglo-Saxon text known today as the *Wonders of the East*. Circulating in both Latin and Old English between c.970–c.1150, the *Wonders* described the marvellous creatures and races of humans that lived on distant continents. Among the phenomena described in the *Wonders* are dog-headed men called cynocephali; ants as big as dogs; giants; a land infested with 150-foot dragons; men with heads in their chests called blemmyae (4); polyglot man-eaters called donestre (5); and griffins, with eagle heads, bovine tails and lion's feet.

Medieval people did not merely want to read about these monstrous races and beasts in ancient texts: they wanted to see pictures of them as well. Illustrated copies

5. *A donestre devours human remains.* England, c.1000. Cotton MS Vitellius A XV, f.103v.

of the *Wonders of the East* demonstrate this appetite for images of monsters. Artists had to imagine what these peoples looked like based on literary descriptions, and on other pictures they had seen; consequently, the same text could inspire rather different images. For example, in the *Wonders* there is a description of timid giants with fan-shaped ears so enormous that they use one as a pillow and the other as a blanket, and when frightened they can take an ear in each hand and rapidly flap to safety. Pliny called these creatures panotii. In one Anglo-Saxon manuscript, the artist shows the panotii with giant shell-shaped ears (6). In another *Wonders* manuscript, produced c.1000, the panotii's ears are shown as long snaking protrusions, coiled around their owner's arms (7).

6. A fan-eared panotii. England, c.1000. Cotton MS Vitellius A XV, f.104r.

The monstrous races provided challenging problems for Christian thinkers. Did they really exist? Were they humans, and if so did they have souls? St Augustine of Hippo, writing in the fourth century, expressed measured caution about the monstrous races, writing 'It is not, of course, necessary to believe in all the kinds of men which are said to exist'. Yet Augustine took seriously the question of whether or not monstrous races shared a common ancestry with humans: were they descended from Adam and Eve? He argued that if they were descendants of Adam, they had souls, and were therefore capable of achieving salvation. God, he reasoned, being all-knowing and all-powerful must have created these monsters for some divine purpose: 'it ought not to seem absurd to us,' he wrote, 'that just as some monsters occur within the various races of mankind, so there should be certain monstrous races within the human race as a whole'. Consequently, Augustine advocated that the monstrous races be treated as wondrous expressions of divine power, provided that they were descended from Adam.

7. A sausage-eared panotii. England (Winchester?), c.1025–1050. Cotton MS Tiberius B V, f.83v.

Despite Augustine's relatively open-minded views about the existence and moral status of monsters, Christian artists nevertheless used monster imagery to demonize foreigners and those of different religions. A good example of this can be found in a Byzantine Psalter copied and illuminated by a monk named Theodore, who completed it in 1066. Throughout the manuscript, Theodore interpreted the verses of the Psalms with images, painted in the margins surrounding the text. One such verse reads 'A pack of dogs surrounds me, a gang of villains is closing in on me' (Psalm 22:16). Theodore

8. *Christ among dog-headed men. Constantinople, 1066.*
Additional MS 19352, f.23r.

interpreted this text by painting Christ surrounded by dog-headed men (cynocephali) with lolling tongues. Inscriptions identify 'Jesus Christ' and the cynocephali are labelled 'Hebrews are dogs'. Thus, through a literal interpretation of the Psalm's words, Theodore characterised the Jews as half-animal monsters (8).

Not all medieval authors and artists shared Theodore's negative view of the monstrous races. Many, following St Augustine's logic that if these races were descended from Adam they must have souls, believed that Christian missionaries had a responsibility to reach out to them whether or not they were physically aberrant. Whether inspired by missionary zeal or simple curiosity, it is clear that many people marvelled at the very idea of the monstrous races. This fascination often took pictorial form, with images of monsters sometimes appearing in surprising places. For example, the final folio of an enormous Bible made at the Premonstratensian Abbey of Arnstein in Germany was left blank by its scribes and illuminators. Taking

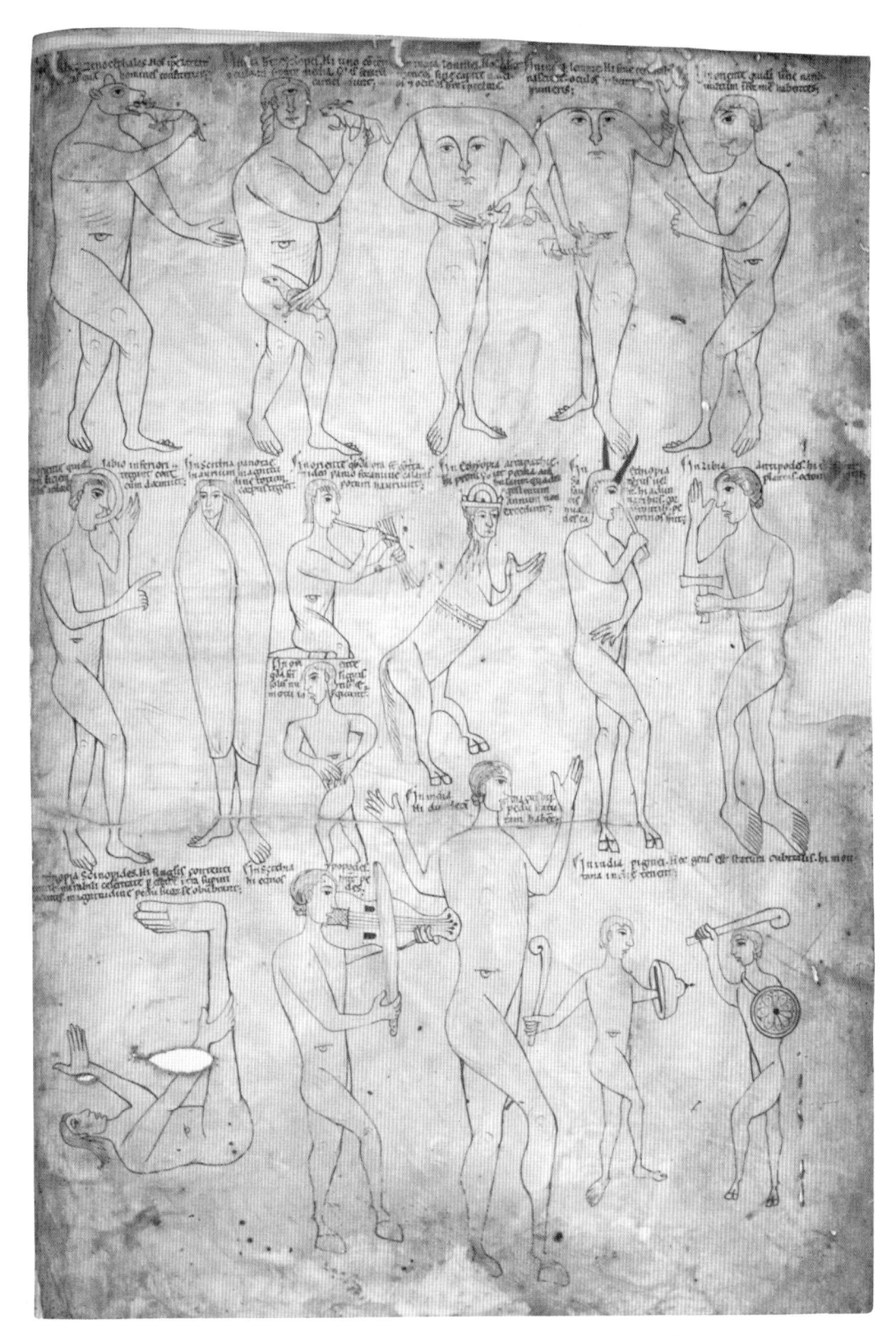

9. Seventeen monstrous races. Germany (Arnstein), c.1175. Harley MS 2799, f.243r.

10. *A map of the world, with Jerusalem at the centre and the monstrous races on the outermost edge. England, c.1265. Additional MS 28681, f.9r.*

11. Detail of the monstrous races. England, c.1265. Additional MS 28681, f.9r.

advantage of the giant parchment page (each page is more than half a metre tall), someone – presumably one of the monks – drew seventeen monstrous humans (9). Blemmyae, sciopods, giants and the cannibalistic donestre parade across the page.

A Christian view of the monstrous races is represented on a miniature map of the world in a diminutive Psalter manuscript made in England around 1265 (10). Like a modern map, this map shows continents, oceans, mountains, rivers and cities, with minute labels written in Latin to identify each feature. But this map is more than a schematic representation of physical geography: it is no less than a map of the spiritual geography of medieval Christendom. Christ stands watching over the world from a heavenly vantage point, holding an orb (itself a symbol of the world) and making a sign of blessing, against a deep blue background flecked with a pattern of white star-like dots, flanked by two angels swinging incense-burners. Two dragons sit at the bottom of the page, crouching as if crushed by the weight of the world. If Christ and the angels symbolise heaven, then the dragons suggest hell, their wings a sinister echo of the angels' wings above. Jerusalem, the holiest of cities, is the very centre of the world. On the right side of the map, perched on the eastern edge of the world, are fourteen tiny images – each no more than one centimetre tall – that show the monstrous races (11).

The edge of the medieval European world was perforated by trade routes, missionary activity and warfare throughout the Middle Ages, but travel to foreign lands appears to have done little to convince anyone that monsters did not really

12. Alexander and his army attack a tribe of cyclopes. N. France or S. Netherlands, c.1290. Harley MS 4979, f.72v.

inhabit the edges of civilisation: in fact, the reverse seems to have been true. Some monsters seem to have roots in real creatures and people, transformed by exaggeration, misunderstanding and distortion through re-telling. Literary accounts of foreign lands were another source of monster lore. Among these, arguably the most influential were the tales of Alexander the Great, who established a vast empire stretching from modern-day Greece, Turkey and Egypt to India in the fourth century B.C.

Alexander's triumphant sweep across Europe, the Middle East and Asia combines the fascination of history, romance and travelogue. Stories of his deeds were told and re-told throughout the Middle Ages, undergoing constant modification and embellishment. Particularly from the twelfth century, readers enthusiastically devoured tales of his adventures, seeing in Alexander the ultimate knight in shining armour. Medieval authors, illuminators and readers were impressed not only by Alexander's military successes against enemy armies, but also the strange and monstrous people and animals that he encountered, and killed, on his campaigns. In these tales, Alexander brings civilisation to wild, untamed lands; his monstrous foes represent the uncivilised, alien worlds he seeks to liberate. Many, if not most, of Alexander's encounters with monsters are overtly bloodthirsty; so, too, are the illustrations that accompany many of the medieval Alexander texts. Made for

13. *Dragons, crabs, and a tri-horned beast are killed by Alexander. Scenes from the romances of Alexander.* France (Rouen), c.1445. Royal MS 15 E VI, ff.15v–16r.

aristocratic patrons as well as more ordinary people, these copies vary in quality, but they are remarkably consistent in their interest in blood and violence.

In a thirteenth-century manuscript of the Alexander romances, the text is punctuated with illustrative miniatures. In one, Alexander and his army charge at a throng of giant cyclopes, who glare at them with their single unblinking eyes (12). Although the cyclopes look ferocious with their massive green clubs, they are doomed, just like all of Alexander's foes. A series of miniatures showing the defeat of a succession of monsters can be seen in a single opening of a lavishly illustrated version of the romance of Alexander (13), part of a volume commissioned as a wedding present for Margaret of Anjou and King Henry VI by John Talbot, 1st Earl of Shrewsbury, in 1445. A swarm of dragons, giant crabs, and a toothy tri-horned beast are all dispatched by Alexander's mighty spear.

A significant exception to Alexander's slaughter of monsters is embodied in the story of his aerial flight. Showing somewhat more curiosity than in other episodes, Alexander decides that he wants to fly into the heavens. Thus, he contrives to catch four griffins. Terrifying and fierce, griffins had the claws and body of a lion, twinned with the beak and wings of an eagle. Despite their viciousness, Alexander easily catches them, harnesses them to a carriage, and climbs inside. Using raw meat on long spears to tempt them (the monstrous equivalent of a carrot dangling on a stick), he prompts the griffins to take flight, carrying him with them (14). Alexander's monster-powered flight was a popular subject in medieval art, provoking wonder in its viewers.

14. *Griffins, enticed by raw meat, carry Alexander into the sky.* N. France or Flanders, c.1300–1310. Royal 20 A V, f.70v.

15. Oedipus encounters the ferocious Sphinx. Latin Kingdom of Jerusalem (Acre), c.1286. Additional MS 15268, f.77v.

The Alexander romances are a tapestry of history, myth and romance. This combination of historical fact and time-honoured fiction appealed hugely to the medieval imagination. *The Universal History* is witness to this appetite: weaving classical myth, ancient history and biblical history together, the text relates the history of the world from its creation to the era of Julius Caesar. Like the Alexander romances, the *Universal History* lends an air of historical authenticity to its more improbable episodes, including its tales of monsters. One of these stories, illustrated in a copy of the *Universal History* made at Acre during the Latin occupation of the Holy Land, is that of Oedipus and the Sphinx (15). In the story, Oedipus encounters a ferocious Sphinx on his way to Thebes. The Sphinx, with the body of a lion and the head of a woman, gives Oedipus a riddle and threatens that if he cannot solve it she will devour him. Oedpius defeats the Sphinx with wit: he solves the riddle, and the Sphinx, in despair, throws

16. Cannibalistic giants and blemmyae as seen by Sir John Mandeville on his travels. England, c.1430. Harley MS 3954, f.42r.

herself over a cliff. In the image, however, Oedipus rides towards the Sphinx, ready to plunge his spear into her chest.

Pliny's *Natural History*, the writings of Herodotus, the *Wonders of the East*, the Alexander romances and the *Universal History* all purport to relate accurate information about faraway lands and the peoples and creatures inhabiting them. In the fourteenth century, a travelogue was penned which continued this venerable tradition. The author of the text described himself as Sir John Mandeville, a knight from St Albans, though this is now generally believed to have been a literary conceit on the part of its author, in all probability a Frenchman. Just as the ancient authors had done before, the fictive Mandeville insisted that he had travelled to distant lands and seen monstrous creatures with his own eyes. The importance of his role as an eye-witness is emphasized in the illustrations to an extraordinary copy of his *Travels*, made in England in about 1430. The oblong shape of this book has prompted some scholars to suggest that the manuscript was intended to be carried in a holster by its owner, and that it may even have accompanied someone on a journey to the lands it describes, functioning as a rather sensational *Rough Guide*. Would its owner have been disappointed not to find the cannibals, blemmyae and other dangerous creatures Mandeville describes (16)? On one page, the illustrator has pictured three naked cannibals, one of whom is seated on the ground as it devours a human leg. The lower miniatures show blemmyae; seated on the ground beside them is Mandeville himself, writing down what he sees. The reader is thus encouraged to believe Mandeville, no matter how incredible his claims, on the grounds that he has seen the marvels he describes with his own eyes.

There were other genres to which medieval marvel-seekers could turn to find out about monsters. Chief among these was the Bestiary, a type of manuscript which flourished in twelfth- and thirteenth-century England. The Bestiary is a moralized encyclopedia of animals, and it includes both fantastical and real creatures. Elephants, wolves, eagles and leopards appear in Bestiaries alongside mythical beasts, such as unicorns, mermaids, satyrs and dragons. The line between monsters and non-monsters is blurred in the Bestiary, as many 'real' creatures are credited with monstrous powers, and many of its monsters are clearly based on ordinary animals such as snakes and lizards. The presence of everyday animals, such as sheep, goats and pigs, might have lent some credibility to the more extraordinary or unfamiliar creatures. Further, it is possible that someone living in England in the twelfth century could have found whales and lions as

17. A crocodile inadvertently swallows a hydrus, which bursts through its side. England (Salisbury?), c.1230–1240. Harley MS 4751, f.62v.

incredible as griffins and mermaids. While in some sense the Bestiary can be seen as a foretaste of what grew, over the centuries, into natural history, the ultimate purpose of the Bestiary was to explore divine truth through the interpretation of the natural world.

Arranged in chapters, the Bestiary explains each animal's behaviour symbolically. One chapter, for example, describes the hydrus, a serpentine creature that lives in the Nile. Above all else, it despises crocodiles: whenever it spies one sleeping on the riverbank with its mouth agape, the hydrus rolls in mud to make itself more slippery, then slides down the crocodile's throat. Startled awake, the crocodile then gulps down the hydrus, who burrows through the crocodile's belly and emerges from its side, killing the crocodile. This process is illustrated in a Bestiary made in England in the 1230s (17). In the image, most of the hydrus is concealed in the body of the crocodile, but the tip of a wing and a slender knotted tail protrudes from the crocodile's mouth. The crocodile's sharp teeth and claws are impotent against the cunning hydrus, whose tail sticks out of the crocodile's mouth as its head emerges from the crocodile's side. The accompanying text likens the crocodile to Death, and the hydrus to Christ: just as the hydrus defeated the crocodile, Christ defied death. The hydrus's attack on the crocodile is also likened to the Harrowing of Hell, when Christ broke down the doors of hell to rescue Adam and Eve.

18. A fire-breathing dragon menaces an elephant. England, c.1255–1265. Harley MS 3244, f.39v.

The Bestiary's account of the hydrus and the crocodile pits a real animal against a fantastical creature. This pairing is found in another section, which concerns the deadly antipathy between the elephant and the dragon. Despite its relative size, the elephant is vulnerable to the dragon, which attacks it with its tail and then suffocates it. However, the Bestiary explains, dragons are afraid of deep water: therefore, the elephant gives birth in a pool of water to protect its offspring. A confrontation between a dragon and an elephant is illustrated in a Bestiary made between 1255 and 1265 (18). The elephant's red-rimmed eyes are wide with terror as the fire-breathing dragon approaches. In this story, the elephant and the dragon represent, respectively, Good and Evil.

The dragon and the hydrus conform to a view of monsters which sees them as frightening, dangerous, and even ugly. Though most monsters were, in some sense, dangerous, not all were frightening and ugly; indeed, some monsters in medieval manuscripts are undeniably beautiful. Perhaps the most famous of these is the unicorn. Too quick for even the fastest hunter, the unicorn could only be caught by a virgin. The unicorn's horn was greatly prized for its magical properties, notably its power to purify poisoned water. It is possible that the unicorn's twisting horn was based on the single tusk of the narwhal, specimens of which might occasionally have washed ashore or even been caught by fishermen in the north seas. The diminutive unicorn was thought to fight elephants, and to defeat them by spearing their bellies. In a Bestiary made in the 1220s for the Benedictine Cathedral Priory at Rochester, a grimacing knight thrusts his spear into the side of a unicorn, who lies with its head on the lap of a naked virgin (19). There is a certain menace in the juxtaposition of the unicorn's horn with the virgin's exposed flesh, though it is unclear whether she ought to be more frightened of the unicorn or the knight who kills it.

The unicorn is more or less benign, but it has a fierce cousin: the monoceros. This creature has an equine body, elephant's feet, the tail of a stag, and a giant horn protruding from the middle of its forehead. Beneath an illustration of a monoceros in a manuscript made c.1230–1240, it is described as 'a monster with a horrible howl' (20). The reader is cautioned that though the monoceros might be killed, it is never captured alive, thanks to its sharp four-foot horn.

19. *A knight spears a unicorn who lies with its head in the lap of a naked virgin.* England (Rochester), c.1220–1240. Royal MS 12 F XIII, f.10v.

Monsters, on the whole, look hideous, their outward ugliness a cipher for inward moral corruption. There are, however some monsters that are dangerously beautiful. Chief among these is the siren; the powerful centaur is, arguably, another. Sirens and centaurs are treated together in the Bestiary, as demonstrated by an accompanying illustration in a continental Bestiary made towards the end of the twelfth century (21). The siren of antiquity had the head of a woman and the body of a bird; during the Middle Ages, this creature was merged with a fish-tailed humanoid, the mermaid, and her mate, the merman. According to ancient legend, the siren lulls sailors into a heavy sleep with her beautiful song; then she pulls them from their ships and tears them to pieces. The medieval imagination was, among other things, enormously practical: it probably made more sense to give this seafaring monster a body to match, allowing her to retain her enchanting birdsong. In the Bestiary image, the siren drags an oarsman over the side of

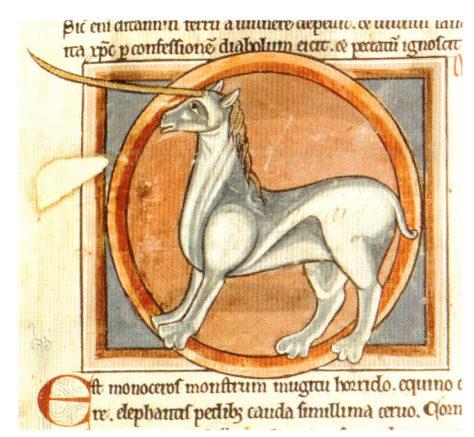

20. *A monoceros. England (Salisbury?), c.1230–1240. Harley MS 4751, f.15r.*

21. *A siren drags a sailor from his boat by the hair; on the right, a centaur fires an arrow. France or Flanders, c.1280–1300. Sloane MS 278, f.47r.*

leçons du serpent a ome et la feme ʃeſ la. b. xj.

E n ſain deulz deux. ceſt aſſan
Adam et eue eſtoient nus
ſi nen eſtoient point hõteux
Et li ſerpens eſtoit la plus
mahaeuſe beſte de toutes lē
beſtes de terre que nre ſire dieu auoit

his boat by the hair. His eyes are wide open (perhaps with shock), but his companions doze, unaware of their friend's fate. Below this scene is an onocentaur, a medieval variation on the ancient centaur, which has the torso of a man and the body of a donkey. In the miniature accompanying the siren, the well-endowed onocentaur has apparently just discharged an arrow from his bow. Both the siren and the centaur are overtly sexual creatures (the artist has particularly emphasized this in the case of the centaur), who ensnare human souls with their powers of attraction.

In the Bestiary, monsters (and other animals) are viewed through an emphatically Christian lens. Many of the Bestiary monsters were inherited from ancient cultures (including the hydrus, unicorn, siren and centaur), but reinvented as expressions of Christian thought and belief. One of the most important sources of medieval thinking about monsters was, inevitably, the Bible. The monsters of the Bible are few, but important: the first is the serpent who tempts Adam and Eve to eat the forbidden fruit, resulting in their expulsion from Paradise. Generally interpreted to be the Devil in disguise, in several ways this serpent is the archetype for demonic monsters of the Middle Ages. Its snaking body a kind of metaphor for opportunistic cunning, the serpent is able to prey on human weaknesses such as pride and greed. In a *Bible Historiale* once owned by the Duc de Berry, the serpent has paws and a fox-like face (22). Eve, clutching leaves to conceal her nudity, hands the forbidden fruit to Adam. Sometimes the serpent is depicted with a woman's head, giving a feminine face to Evil.

Dragons and other monstrous beasts appear in abundance in the final book of the Bible, the Revelation of St John, also known as the Apocalypse. This book recounts St John's prophetic vision of the end of the world, describing the events leading up to the second coming of Christ and the Last Judgement. Rich in enigmatic symbols which defy easy explanation, St John describes how cataclysmic events are unleashed upon the world, including floods, plagues, earthquakes and falling stars. The advancing destruction of the Apocalypse is signalled by the reversal of nature. Monstrous creatures are a potent expression of the apocalyptic world. Beasts with multiple heads, plagues of insects and frogs, and demons with supernatural powers were depicted alongside the text of Revelation.

A plague of locusts is among those prophesied by Revelation, which describes how ordinary locusts are made monstrous during the Apocalypse: given the power to sting like scorpions, human-looking faces and women's hair topped with golden

22. *The serpent tempts Adam and Eve; a decorative dragon embellishes the lower border.*
France, c.1403. Harley MS 4381, f.8r.

23. An apocalyptic plague of human-headed locusts. France, 1380s. Yates Thompson MS 10, f.14v.

crowns, and arrayed like warhorses, the locusts are sent forth to torture sinners and non-believers. In an English copy of the Apocalypse, the artist has vividly portrayed the advancing swarm of human-headed locusts, their leader behind them (23). Another Apocalypse manuscript, made in England c.1310–1325, shows St John as an eye witness to monstrous events: in one image, he watches, book in hand, as frogs emerge from the mouths of a seven-headed dragon, a seven-headed beast and false prophets (24).

The beasts witnessed by St John were evocative symbols of the corrupting power of the Devil, and the spiritual consequences of succumbing to evil. In a copy of *La Somme le Roy*, a treatise on morality written for the King of France by a Dominican Friar, the many-headed beast of the Apocalypse appears in a full-page frontispiece miniature (25). Painted by the hugely influential Parisian illuminator, Maître Honoré, the image shows the monster with seven heads surmounted by ten crowns trampling a saint as a hypocrite kneels down before it. The inscription in red above the image reads 'Cest beste senefie le deable': the beast signifies the Devil. Below, the caption describes how the beast tramples the saint as the hypocrite prays to it.

MONSTERS AND GROTESQUES IN MEDIEVAL MANUSCRIPTS

24. St John witnesses frogs emerging from the mouths of a many-headed dragon, a seven-headed beast, and false prophets. England, c.1310–1325.
Royal MS 19 B XV, f.30v.

25. A hypocrite kneels before a satanic beast as it tramples a saint.
France (Paris), 1290s.
Additional MS 54180, f.14v.

26. St Michael and an army of angels battle a many-headed beast.
Spain (Silos), c.1073–1109.
Additional MS 11695, ff.147v–148r.

ubi draco cum xia
tereg; cum pu ta in
saeclu ru m

draco cum xia angelis hih ptae in uno cum a

In Revelation, one of the central dramas of Christianity unfolds: the battle between Good and Evil. Evil, unsurprisingly, is embodied by explicitly monstrous forms. One of the most dramatic episodes in Revelation is the battle between St Michael, assisted by an army of angels, and Satan:

> *And now war broke out in heaven, when Michael with his angels attacked the dragon. The dragon fought back with his angels, but they were defeated and driven out of heaven. The great dragon, the primeval serpent, known as the devil or Satan, who had led all the world astray, was hurled down to the earth and his angels were hurled down with him.*
>
> Revelation 12:7–9

In the Silos Apocalypse, the image of encounter between St Michael and the 'primeval serpent' is dominated by the seven-headed beast, whose serpentine tail is knotted like a pretzel (26). Made at the monastery of Silos in Spain between c.1073–1109, the importance of this scene is emphasized by the double-page opening devoted to it. In the image, an army of angels attacks a beast with seven heads and ten horns, which the accompanying text explains is the Devil.

The image of St Michael battling the dragon was a powerful evocation of the spiritual battle between Good and Evil, and a potent reminder that Christians could call upon the saints to help them in their own struggles. In the Tiberius Psalter, one of the supreme survivals of Anglo-Saxon manuscript illumination, an image of St Michael spearing the dragon appears as one of a sequence of images concerning the triumph of Good over Evil. The manuscript was damaged in a fire in 1731, but nevertheless it is possible to make out the inscription at the top of the page, which labels the monster 'dracone', or dragon (27). So potent was this image of the confrontation between Good and Evil that a viewer physically attacked the image of the dragon, leaving small irregular slashes in the surface of the page. Indeed, every image representing evil in the Psalter has been treated the same way, with small yet distinct scratches piercing the parchment page. This kind of defacement is common in medieval manuscripts, where the faces of evil-doers (particularly the tormentors of Christ), devils and demons frequently show signs of being smudged or scratched. It is impossible to say whether these marks were made out of a superstitious belief that images of evil creatures themselves had evil powers, or as a emotional reaction to the image's message about good and evil.

27. St Michael kills a dragon. England (Winchester), c.1050. Cotton MS Tiberius C VI, f.16r.

It is interesting to compare the Tiberius Psalter's dragon with a sea monster drawn by an Anglo-Saxon artist working in France c.1000, about fifty years before the Tiberius Psalter was made (28). If classical antiquity had given the Middle Ages a world teeming with monstrous races and creatures, it also bequeathed to medieval astronomy and astrology a monster-studded view of the heavens. Among the gods

28. *A diagram of the constellation of the sea monster Cetus. France, late 10th century. Harley MS 2506, f.42r.*

and heroes in the constellations were monstrous beasts. A manuscript made at the monastery of Fleury includes excerpts from an astronomical treatise called the *De Signis Caeli*. The constellation Cetus (whose name, in Latin, means whale), the sea monster whose attempt to devour Andromeda was thwarted by Perseus, is shown with a twisting tail, claws and a lolling, pointed tongue. The stellar points of the constellation are shown as red dots. Cetus and the Tiberius Psalter dragon are strikingly similar, no doubt due to the common heritage of the artists. That they should be so alike, despite the differences in context, suggests that a medieval viewer familiar with the standard portrayal of St Michael's dragon might overlay the image of Cetus with Christian significance; so, too, might the viewer transpose antique meanings onto the Apocalyptic dragon.

The dragon's evil connotations made it an ideal enemy for saints. The Virgin often tramples a dragon underfoot, while other saints were particularly known as dragon-slayers. Most famous of these was St George, a warrior saint who was venerated widely in Europe throughout the Middle Ages (29). St Margaret employed different methods to triumph over a dragon: her legend recounts that while praying, she was eaten by a dragon and escaped by using the cross in her hand to cut her way

29. St George kills a dragon. France, c.1370–1390. Additional MS 23145, f.36r.

30. St Margaret bursts through the belly of a dragon. England, c.1270. Additional MS 48985, f.124v.

through its belly. An historiated initial in the Salvin Hours shows her emerging from a gash in its side before the dragon has even finished devouring her skirts. Her hands pressed together prayerfully, and a divine hand blesses her from the heavens (30).

Apocryphal Biblical texts recounted how Satan had once been an angel named Lucifer who had rebelled against God. He and his supporters were expelled from heaven, and so became the antithesis of the angels they had once been: the angel Lucifer was thus transformed into Satan, and the rebel angels became demons. Cast down into hell, this army of demons, devils and monstrous creatures had tempted, tricked and tormented men and women from the beginning of time. The Devil, in the guise of a serpent, had convinced Eve to sample the fruit of the forbidden tree, prompting the expulsion of Adam and Eve from the Garden of Eden. In the New Testament, Satan appeared to Jesus during his forty days in the wilderness, evidence that no-one – not even Christ himself – was safe from the Devil's attempts to corrupt human souls. But, unlike Adam and Eve, Jesus resisted the Devil's advances; thus, images of Christ being tempted by Satan would have inspired viewers to follow Christ's example. In their depictions of devils and demons, medieval artists made them as ghastly as possible. Covered with hair, medieval demons grin and snarl; they often have pig-like snouts, asinine ears and tails, and frequently grotesque faces stare out of their bellies and bottoms.

31. Opposite page: The damned are swallowed by a hell-mouth. England (Winchester), 1220s. Cotton MS Nero C IV, f.39r.

ICI EST ENFERS E LI ANGELS KI ENFERME LES PORTES

Throngs of demonic monsters inhabit hell in medieval art. Hell itself is often shown as a monster, with a giant mouth devouring human souls. In the Winchester Psalter, made in England at Winchester in the 1220s, a bestial hell-mouth is stuffed with human bodies (31). Inside the toothy mouth, demons torture damned souls. With furry faces, human bodies and feline claws, many of these demons grin and laugh as they torment their victims. One demon shakes a crowned man upside down, while elsewhere a lion-tailed demon spears an upside-down king with a pitchfork. On the left, an angel turns a key in the gate of hell, locking the damned souls in hell for eternity.

Depictions of the Last Judgement reminded medieval Christians of the test that awaited them at death: if they passed, they could spend eternity among the angels in paradise, but if they failed, among the fiends of hell. In the Holkham Bible Picture Book, made in England c.1320, Christ sits in Judgement over human souls (32). On his right (the left of the page), next to an angel holding the cross and nails of the crucifixion, stand the elect, those whose souls have been saved. In the lower register of the image, the saved souls, shown as naked people, are ushered by angels through the gates of paradise as heavenly music is played by other angels. On the opposite side of the page, at Christ's left hand, are the damned. Bound with a rope, they are led away by a fiend with a cruel grimace, long pointed ears and an up-turned pig-like snout. Among them are monks, with their hair trimmed into a monastic tonsure, a crowned queen and a bishop wearing a mitre. The message here is clear: no sinner will be spared God's wrath, not even the wealthiest and most powerful. Below, doomed souls are roasted in cauldrons over a fiery hell-mouth, as damned souls are added to the conflagration by the cart-load.

The *Divine Comedy* of Dante Alighieri is surely the most powerful literary evocation of the medieval conception of hell. Written in the early fourteenth century in the author's native Italian, Dante narrates a dream-vision in which he travels through hell, purgatory and paradise. With the ancient poet Virgil as his guide, Dante descends into hell, a vast chasm in the centre of the earth. Dante vividly describes hell's deformed and tortured souls, who recount the earthly sins for which they are being punished. Some he recognises, and many others are anonymous sinners. At the very bottom of hell, Dante and Virgil encounter Satan himself. Frozen with terror at the sight, Dante describes him as 'the emperor of the kingdom of pain'. As

32. Christ sits in judgement over human souls: the elect enter heaven, while the damned are dragged to hell. England, c.1320–1330. Additional MS 47682, f.42v.

demonically ugly as he once was angelically beautiful, Dante's Satan is a giant with bat wings and three faces, chewing a sinner with each of his three mouths. In a copy of the *Divine Comedy* made and illustrated c.1370 in Naples, the artist has illustrated this passage with an image of Dante and Virgil climbing up Satan's leg (33).

The physical and spiritual danger posed by demons, and the power that saints had to defeat them is the subject of many images in medieval manuscripts. The most powerful saint of all was the Virgin Mary. She is frequently shown trampling on the Devil. At the bottom of a page in the Queen Mary Psalter, probably made in London c.1320, the evil nature of the Devil and the power of the Virgin to defeat him is expressed in a single scene. A demon is shown drowning a monk. He stands on a bridge and holds the monk by the ankles. But the monk prays to the Virgin, who rescues him (34).

33. Dante and Virgil scale Satan's furry leg. Italy (Naples), c.1370. Additional MS 19587, f.58r.

Medieval commentators, keen to moralize, frequently interpreted outward, physical deformity as a sign of inner, moral corruption. The human status of the monstrous races was compromised by their lack of Christian faith, while dragons, serpents and reptiles were likened to the satanic serpent who tempted Eve in the Garden of Eden. But medieval artists understood that monsters were not just useful objects for moralization: they could also be entertaining, both by thrilling viewers with the electric *frisson* that people seek today in horror films, and through their comic absurdity. The comic potential of monsters, like so much else, was considered by antique authors. In his treatise on the *Arts of Poetry* (written c.10 B.C.), the Roman author Horace described the ability of the artist to make people laugh with ridiculous creatures:

34. The intercession of the Virgin Mary saves a monk from a murderous demon. England (London?), c.1310–1320. Royal MS 2 B VII, f.213v.

> Supposing a painter chose to put a human head on a horse's neck, or to spread feathers of various colours over the limbs of several different creatures, or to make what in the upper part is a beautiful woman tail off into a hideous fish: could you help laughing when he showed you his efforts?

In a twelfth-century copy of this text, an artist has responded to this introductory passage by drawing the sort of fantastical creature described by Horace (35). In this context, the hybrid monster is tethered to a literary source; increasingly, in ensuing

35. A comical hybrid illustrates the opening lines of Horace's Ars Poetica. Germany, c.1175–1200. Royal MS 15 B VII, f.3v.

decades and centuries, monsters began to appear in margins and borders of manuscripts without literary provocation.

Popular in manuscripts produced all over Europe, enthusiasm for marginal monsters was nowhere stronger than in England, France and the Netherlands. Creeping out of the letter-forms they had long inhabited, dragons became conspicuous in margins. Mermaids, centaurs and griffins became entwined in borders. The new prominence of these monsters was not confined to manuscripts: stained glass, architectural sculpture, small ivories, enamels and other art forms all bear witness to the increasing popularity of monstrous images. Yet not everyone approved of the ubiquity of these images. Writing early in the 1120s, St Bernard of Clairvaux, the powerful Abbot of the Cistercian order, penned a scathing attack on these creatures, and in doing so left an evocative description of what he saw:

> *What excuse can there be for these ridiculous monstrosities in the cloisters where the monks do their reading, extraordinary things at once beautiful and ugly? Here we find filthy monkeys and fierce lions, fearful centaurs, harpies, and striped tigers... Here is one head with many bodies, there is one body with many heads. Over there is a beast with a serpent for its tail, a fish with an animal's head, and a creature that is horse in front and goat behind, and a second beast with horns and the rear of a horse.*

St Bernard was not the only writer to rail against the profusion of monstrous imagery. Self-consciously echoing St Bernard's words, the anonymous English author of a treatise on painting, the *Pictor in Carmine* (c.1200) denounced the 'misshapen monstrosities' decorating the sacred spaces near the altar, proclaiming that the 'double-headed eagles, four lions with one and the same head, centaurs with quivers, [and] headless men grinning' ought to be replaced with more edifying images. Yet despite the fervour of their words, these authors' protests would seem to have been in vain: the very creatures they describe can be found in abundance, decorating not only churches, but also manuscripts containing sacred texts.

St Bernard's denunciation of monstrous images is part of a longer text addressed to fellow monks in his own order, the Cistercians, and their rivals, the Cluniacs. Historically, most manuscripts would have been made by monks, but by St Bernard's time, developments in medieval society were dramatically changing the ways that manuscripts were produced and the type of people who owned them. From the early Middle Ages, the ability to read and write had largely belonged to monks. But from the twelfth century, laymen and women were learning to read in ever greater numbers. Whereas in the past, book production had been dominated by monasteries, from the thirteenth century it was increasingly possible to commission manuscripts from professional scribes and lay-owned illuminators in towns and cities. Illuminated manuscripts remained prohibitively expensive for all but the wealthiest, so we can be confident that almost all of the illuminated manuscripts that survive belonged to members of the social and economic elite. Monks may have paid some attention to St Bernard's condemnation of unedifying decoration, but the abundance of monsters in medieval manuscripts suggests that lay illuminators and their wealthy patrons did not.

Many terms are used to describe the marginal monsters in medieval manuscripts. Monsters whose bodies are composed of different elements are often referred to as hybrids. These same monsters might have been described in the Middle Ages as chimera. In Greek mythology, the chimera was a fire-breathing monster with a lion's head, goat's body and serpentine tail; by the end of the fourteenth century the word had come to describe similarly hybridized creatures. Gryllus, the Latin word for grasshopper, is sometimes used for marginal creatures made up of legs with faces between them. Comical monsters are sometimes described as drolleries, though this term can apply to other types of amusing marginal images. The Middle English word 'babewyn', the root of the modern English baboon, was used by medieval people to describe the creatures that decorated their books and buildings.

Of these terms, one of the best known is 'grotesque', which appears in the title of this book. In the context of medieval manuscript illumination, grotesques are unnatural combinations of animal, plant and human forms. Unlike 'monster', which medieval people used themselves (in its Latin form or in medieval vernaculars), 'grotesque' is a modern term with an interesting post-medieval pedigree. In 1488, a magnificent palace of the Emperor Nero (d.68 A.D.) was discovered in the caves, called grottoes, on the edge of Rome. The extraordinary decoration of this palace was a source of inspiration for artists, architects and interior designers for centuries afterwards, who were dazzled by the profusion of putti, mythical monsters, trompe-l'oeil architectural forms and floral decoration which embellished its walls and ceilings. Illuminators, too, incorporated antique decorative motifs in the borders, initials and miniatures of manuscripts made for patrons who devoted themselves to classical learning, literature and art. In a Book of Hours made for Bonaparte Ghislieri, a member of a wealthy Bolognese family, the most important pages are decorated with borders inspired by antique decorative arts as found in Nero's palace (36). By the sixteenth century, people had started to use the word grotesque (derived from the word grotto) to describe images containing motifs of classical derivation like the ones found in the Roman grottoes. By the eighteenth century, the term grotesque was applied to marginal ornamentation in manuscripts on the basis of its connection to antique sources. Today, it is a portmanteau term used to describe all kinds of comic, repulsive and absurd decorative imagery in manuscripts.

Grotesques in Gothic manuscripts can be playful, satirical, crude, violent, elegant and overtly sexual. They appear in sumptuous manuscripts for which no expense was spared, as well as in more ordinary books illuminated by artists working at speed. The margins of even the most sacred texts were illuminated with monstrous images. Sometimes the contrast between solemn religious texts and the playful and provocative monsters in the margins beside them is startlingly subversive. What is the cheeky monster doing kneeling over the Psalms in the Gorleston Psalter (37)? In other places, pictures in the margin seem to have nothing to do with the text: why is a knight killing a griffin in the bas-de-page of the Alphonso Psalter (38)? There is no simple answer to these questions. These creatures were clearly intended to be shocking and funny, but more earnest intentions may have been at work as well. These comical and crude hybrids, and their monstrous behaviour, belong to the world of the body and its basest

36. *A border inspired by the kind of grotesque decoration of Nero's Domus Aurea. Italy (Bologna), c.1500. Yates Thompson MS 29, f.16r.*

37. *A hooded hybrid with a splayed bottom perches on an initial. England (Gorleston, Suffolk), c.1310–1335. Additional MS 49622, f.62v.*

functions. Most of the texts they stand next to, by contrast, concern the spirit. The tension between the desires of the body and the needs of the spirit was keenly felt in the Middle Ages: medieval Christians fervently believed that the sins incurred with their mortal flesh would be paid for in eternity by their immortal souls. The farting, naked, and lecherous monsters that swarm in manuscript margins make ordinary human desires seem laughable. Medieval viewers might have laughed at grotesques, but far from promoting the kind of sexualized and corporeal monstrosity they portray, these marginal images might well have served to condemn it with ridicule.

Marginal monsters abound in a Bible copied by a scribe named William of Devon between c.1260–c.1270 (39). The first words of Genesis are 'In principio creavit Deus caelum et terram': In the beginning God created heaven and earth.

38. *A knight kills a griffin, avenging the killing of his horse. England, c.1284. Additional MS 24686, f.18r.*

39. Dragons, hybrids and animals play in margins of the first page of Genesis. England (Oxford?), c.1260–1270. Royal MS 1 D 1, f.5r.

A series of scenes illustrating some of the episodes from Genesis are fitted into the elongated initial 'I' of this first phrase. In the margins surrounding the columns of text, the artist has painted a profusion of comical monsters, cranes, dragons. Hounds chase a stag in the upper margin; an archer shoots a hare on the right side of the page; along the bottom, a dog dressed as a bishop blesses a bird in a friar's cloak; and in all the margins, hooded hybrids interact with long-legged cranes. Perhaps this profusion of animal imagery is a cryptic response to the text, which describes God's creation of the animals. Conversely, it could simply be a way of embellishing the page with entertaining and eye-catching images, signalling to the reader the care and expense that had been lavished upon the volume.

Of the illuminated manuscripts commissioned by lay patrons in the later Middle Ages, Psalters and Books of Hours were the most popular. Psalters normally contain the one hundred and fifty Psalms of the Old Testament, as well as a liturgical calendar. An important part of the monastic and secular liturgy, as well as for private reading and contemplation, until the early fourteenth century, if a family was to own only one book, it would most likely be a Psalter. One such family-owned Psalter is the Luttrell Psalter, made for Sir Geoffrey Luttrell of Irnham in Lincolnshire between c.1325–1335, is celebrated for its profusion of marginal imagery. Many of the images in the Luttrell Psalter depict the routines of daily life on a medieval estate, from tilling the earth and sowing seeds to butchering animals and preparing banquets. Interspersed with these realistic scenes are creatures of such startling monstrosity that they prompted one scholar to comment that 'the mind of a man who could deliberately set himself to ornament a book with such subjects... can hardly have been normal'. While it seems unwise to use the margins of the Luttrell Psalter to diagnose the mental condition of its artists, there can be no doubt that the artist who illuminated many of its pages had an exceptionally fertile imagination.

Grinning and gurning monsters greet the viewer on nearly every page of the Luttrell Psalter. In one opening, a boy is shown stealing cherries from a tree; an exasperated farmer looks up helplessly as his harvest is devoured (40). Looming around this scene in the margins on the same page and opposite, a startling variety of monsters clamour for attention. In the lower border, a creature with a predatory hooked beak and a striped tiger-like body seems to glare across at the cherry stealing scene. In the right vertical margin, an armless hybrid with chicken's feet and a man's

40. *A boy steals cherries; monsters fill the surrounding borders.* England, c.1325–1335. Additional MS 42130, ff.196v–197r.

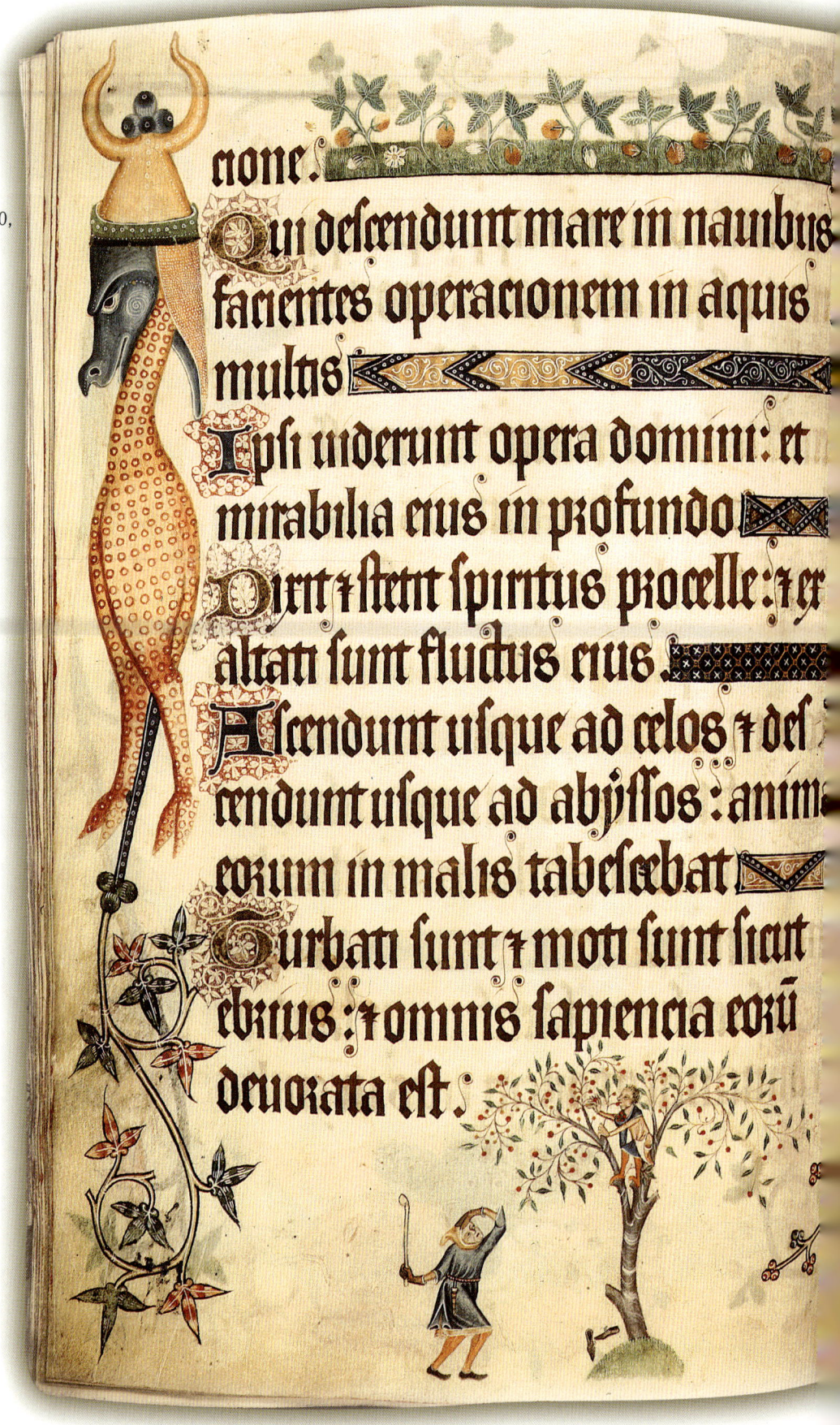

none. Qui descendunt mare in nauibus facientes operacionem in aquis multis

Ipsi uiderunt opera domini: et mirabilia eius in profundo

Dixit & stetit spiritus procelle: & exaltati sunt fluctus eius

Ascendunt usque ad celos & descendunt usque ad abyssos: anima eorum in malis tabescebat

Turbati sunt & moti sunt sicut ebrius: & omnis sapiencia eorum deuorata est

Et clamauerunt ad dominum
cum tribularentur: 7 de necessitati
bus eorum eduxit eos
Et statuit procellam eius in auram:
et siluerunt fluctus eius
Et letati sunt quia siluerunt: 7 de
duxit eos in portum uoluntatis
eorum
Confiteantur domino misericor
die eius:: 7 mirabilia eius filiis ho
minum
Et exaltent eum in ecclesia plebis:
et in cathedra seniorum laudent eu
Posuit flumina in desertum: et

face supports on his shoulders a jester with bells on his hood, who obligingly holds up a bar of foliate border. On the left, a hybrid with cloven hooves and a spotted coat glares off to the side. It seems unlikely that the images are a response to the adjacent text of Psalm 106: 23–33, which is replete with aquatic imagery but mentions neither monsters nor cherries. There may be, however, some link between the marginal images: if the monsters are interpreted as symbols of spiritual monstrosity, then perhaps the image is a warning to the viewer of the dangers of petty thievery and the ubiquity of the Devil.

Grotesques were sometimes deployed by artists in ways that playfully exploited the conventions that governed the design of a page. In the Alphonso Psalter, made in England in c.1284, an illuminator staged a face-off between a lizard and a winged dragon (41). The lizard, shown from a bird's-eye view, is exquisitely drawn in the margin. Its scaly green body is skilfully modelled, and its red tongue flicks out at the small dragon, lodged in the border. This seems like a playful confrontation between a realistic animal and an imaginary beast: the lizard looks able to scamper away but the dragon is stuck, its tail fused to the border. Other grotesques interact directly with the text or other elements of the decoration. On one page of the Bohun Psalter, an English production of the later fourteenth century, a small winged grotesque tugs the border into an interlace pattern (42).

41. *A confrontation between a reptile and a dragon. England, c.1284. Additional MS 24686, f.18v.*

42. *A winged grotesque tugs the foliate border into place. England, between 1361–1373. Egerton MS 3277, f.29v.*

Many of the monsters that inhabit the margins of Gothic manuscripts are familiar from earlier sources. The Rutland Psalter's illuminator clearly had special enthusiasm for the monstrous races. Its margins, illuminated in England c.1250, boast many monsters with a clear pedigree in the Plinian monsters that were included in the *Wonders of the East*, including panotii and blemmyae. On f.87v, an arrow shot from the bow of a hunched creature is about to hit the bottom of a sciopod, who is oblivious to the imminent strike (43).

43. *A web-footed sciopod is shot in the bottom by a hunched man. England, c.1260. Additional MS 62925, f.87v.*

44. Monsters and monkeys ape the Office of the Dead. France (St Omer), 1320s. Additional MS 36684, f.125r.

The Psalter's popularity was gradually eclipsed in the fourteenth century by the Book of Hours, a type of prayer book favoured by laymen and women. Books of Hours normally contained the Hours of the Virgin (a series of prayers recited at nine times throughout the day), a liturgical calendar, as well as other devotional material often including a selection of Psalms, the litany, and prayers to various saints, known as suffrages. As with Psalters, the overtly devotional nature of Books of Hours did not preserve their margins from a parade of grotesques.

Monstrous mockery fills the margins of a small fourteenth-century French Book of Hours. This book includes the Office of the Dead, a solemn text read to pray for the souls of the dead. In the miniature marking the beginning of this text, a group of monks are shown standing at the foot of a coffin draped with a cloth, singing the Office. This earnest scene is parodied by in the chaotic margins by monsters, monkeys, and birds, who imitate the monks pictured in the principal miniature (44). In the miniature, one of the monks holds an open book from which the monks sing. In the margins, similar books flap around, sometimes in the hands of monkeys, consulted by hooved hybrids, or in the beaks of birds. Death itself is mocked by a laughing skeleton and a grave-digging hybrid who trudges along with a shovel over his shoulder. This page is dominated by images: its three lines of text are completely surrounded by the solemn miniature and its marginal inversion.

The human body, deformed and distorted, is frequently the object of monstrous humour in Gothic margins. Monsters which exaggerate the body and its functions appear next to texts concerning sacred teachings, devotion and religious law. As suggested above, this juxtaposition between sacred or spiritual writings and profane images can be seen as an expression of the medieval interest in the division between body and spirit. Bottoms, which belong emphatically to the corporeal realm, were an enduring source of visual humour for medieval illuminators and their patrons. Earlier, we saw a startlingly explicit marginal image from the Gorleston Psalter, showing a hybrid with a human head and splayed male bottom (37). An opening of a tiny Book of Hours made c.1300 in Liège shows a hunchback monster with a human head firing arrows at a monkey mounted on a hybrid, whose rear has been struck and is bleeding profusely (45). One hybrid in the Luttrell Psalter plays the bagpipes with one end and a horn with the other (46). Among the most eye-popping of these monstrous bottoms is an image in a copy of the

MONSTERS AND GROTESQUES IN MEDIEVAL MANUSCRIPTS

45. One hybrid shoots another in the bottom. Flanders (Liege), c.1300. Stowe MS 17, ff.223v–224r.

46. A hybrid plays horns with both ends. England, c.1325–1335. Additional MS 42130, f.185v.

47. One monster licks the bottom of another. England, c.1300. Stowe MS 49, f.65r.

Golden Legend, a collection of saints' lives, which was copied in England in about 1300 by a scribe named Alanus. Alanus seems to have entertained himself by drawing comical scenes in the margins of the text he was copying, including a pair of hybrids, one of which is licking the other's anus (perhaps a pun on Alanus's name?) (47).

It can be difficult to understand the meaning of monsters when they appear without any apparent contextual link to the text. Sometimes, surely, they are simply a playful or mildly subversive expression of artistic (or, in the case of Alanus, scribal) imagination. Sometimes, monsters appear in pictorial narratives; in these instances, their potential meanings are more transparent. One such narrative concerns a wild man, one of the most richly symbolic creatures that inhabits medieval art and literature. The opposite of the civilised man, the wild man wears no clothes, but has a thick, tangled coat of hair; instead of walking upright, he crawls on all fours; he can neither read nor write, and lives in the wilderness. The medieval wild man had roots in the Old Testament story of King Nebuchadnezzer, who was punished for his arrogance by God with a period of insanity, during which he grew bird-like talons, a furry coat, and crawled on his hands and knees. Like Nebuchadnezzer, the wild man was seen as a spiritual exile, usually the victim of his own sin.

48. *A hermit is tempted by a demon. England, c.1340. Royal MS 10 E IV, f.113v.*

In the margins of the Smithfield Decretals, a law book that was illuminated in London c.1340, pictures tell the story of a hermit who is tempted by a fiend to commit deadly sins (48). Versions of this story appear in collections of stories known as *exempla*, which were compiled for preachers to use in their sermons. In these textual versions of the story, the naïve hermit wonders what sin is. In the Smithfield Decretals, he is shown sitting outside his isolated hut, when he is approached by a demon with fierce claws, donkey's ears and a pointed, snake-like tongue. The demon says that he must choose one of three sins: to drink, to fornicate, or to murder. Infected with the demon's amorality, the hermit reasons that the least bad sin is to drink, so he goes to a tavern where he is tempted by the attractive alewife. Drunk and thus incapable of resisting his sinful impulses, he seduces her. A miller spies them and, horrified at being caught, the hermit kills him. Thus, he has committed all three sins. Distraught, the hermit tears off his clothes and flees into the wilderness. There he becomes an animal-like wild man, no longer fully human because of his grievous sins (49). Both the demon and the

49. *Transformed into a wild man, the hermit crawls into a cave. England, c.1340. Royal MS 10 E IV, f.117v.*

wild man are presented as spiritual monsters, their alienation from God's grace represented by their bodily disfigurement. The story concludes with the wild man repenting for his sins; he is restored to his human form, and returns to his life as a hermit.

Another wildman story is related in images in the Taymouth Hours, a small Book of Hours made in England c.1325. A lady, out picking flowers, is attacked by a wild man; she is rescued by a knight (50). This is a story with a twist, however, as the knight proves, ultimately, to be as dangerous as the wild man: when the lady prefers the company of a younger knight, the knight who rescued her responds first by killing her suitor, and then by abandoning her in the wilderness.

In both of these stories, the wild man's animal appearance reflects his inner moral state: irrational, uncivilized, and (most importantly) in a state of sin. They warn that ordinary people can become outwardly monstrous through sin, but also that this state can be reversed through penitence. Reflecting on the other monsters we have encountered in medieval manuscripts, this thematic concern with

50. *Above:* A wild man lays dying as a knight comforts a lady. *Opposite:* Two knights struggle over the lady. England, c.1325–1335. Yates Thompson MS 13, ff.63v–64r.

morality underpins many of them. Of course, not all medieval monsters were intended to be morally improving, but each deserves to be considered in the light of the long tradition to which it belongs; in this way, hidden or obscure meanings can become apparent.

It is a testament to the longevity of antique and medieval monsters that they endure to this day, reinvented for the modern age in movies, comic books, novels, and video games. Medieval sea monsters have an heir in the great white shark of *Jaws*; dragons evolved into the intergalactic monsters of the *Alien* films; unicorns and centaurs gallop in the forests of *Harry Potter*. Perhaps just as every age needs knights in shining armour, so too it needs fire-breathing dragons. We share with our medieval ancestors many of the same fears: the dark, lonely wildernesses, strangers, dangerous creatures, things that go bump in the night. So, too, do we share a desire to transform these fears into thrilling and terrifying tales, enjoying the cathartic thrill of cinematic horror as much as medieval people must once have enjoyed hearing of cannibals, vicious reptiles and cunning demons.

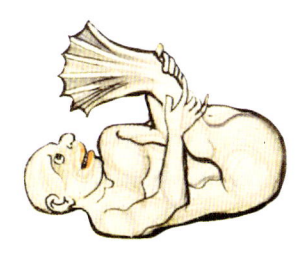

FURTHER READING

For general introductions to medieval beasts, see John Cherry, ed., *Mythical Beasts* (London, 1995) and Ann Payne, *Medieval Beasts* (London, 1991). John Block Friedman's *The Monstrous Races in Medieval Art and Thought* is the most comprehensive introduction to the monstrous races, tracing their history from antiquity to the late Middle Ages (Cambridge, Massachusetts, 1981; reprinted with up-to-date bibliography: Syracuse, New York, 2000). Rudolf Wittkower's 'Marvels of the East: A Study on the History of Monsters' remains a fundamental introduction to the monstrous races (*Journal of the Warburg and Courtauld Institutes* 5, 1942, pp.159–197; reprinted in *Allegory and the Migration of Symbols*, New York, 1987, pp.45–74). The best recent study of Bestiaries is Ron Baxter, *Bestiaries and their Users in the Middle Ages* (Gloucester, 1998), which includes a useful précis and critique of Bestiary scholarship, as well as an extensive bibliography. Lilian Randall's *Images in the Margins of Gothic Manuscripts* includes an excellent introduction and provides illustrations of an impressive range of hybrids and monsters (Berkeley, California, 1966). Among the most influential recent studies of medieval marginalia is Michael Camille, *Image on the Edge: The Margins of Medieval Art* (London, 1992). Recent publications with a theoretical and psychoanalytic interest in medieval monsters include David Williams, *Deformed Discourse: The Function of the Monster in Mediaeval Thought and Literature* (Exeter, 1996) and Jeffrey Cohen, *Of Giants: Sex, Monsters, and the Middle Ages* (Minneapolis, Minnesota, 1999). For most of the English manuscripts mentioned here, see the volumes of *A Survey of Manuscripts Illuminated in the British Isles*, 6 vols. (London, 1978–1996), gen. ed. J.J.G. Alexander.

PUBLISHED SOURCES QUOTED

Sir John Mandeville's definition of a monster: *The Travels of Sir John Mandeville: The version of the Cotton Manuscript in modern spelling*, ed. A.W. Pollard (London, 1900), p.32.

St Augustine's discussion of the monstrous races: St Augustine of Hippo, *The City of God Against the Pagans*, ed. Robert Dyson (Cambridge, 1998), pp.707–710 (book XVI, chapter 8).

The remark about the Luttrell Psalter ('The mind of the man …'): E.G. Millar, ed., *The Luttrell Psalter* (London, 1932), p.16.

St Bernard of Clairvaux's denunciation of monstrous images: Michael Casey, trans., *Cistercians and Cluniacs: St Bernard's Apologia to Abbot William* (Kalamazoo, Michigan, 1970), book XII, Chapter 29, pp.66–67.

The anonymous treatise of c.1200 echoing St Bernard's views on monstrous imagery: M.R. James, 'Pictor in Carmine', *Archaeologia* 94 (1951), pp.141–166.

Quotations from the Bestiary: T.H. White, *The Book of Beasts* (London, 1954; reprinted Gloucester, 1984).

The opening lines of Horace's *Ars Poetica*: Horace, *On the Art of Poetry*, in *Classical Literary Criticism*, trans. T.S. Dorsch (Harmondsworth, 1965), p.79.

Dante's description of Satan: Dante Alighieri, *The Divine Comedy*, trans. C.H. Sisson (Oxford, 1980), Inferno Canto XXXIV, p.191.

Biblical quotations are taken from the New Jerusalem Version.

MANUSCRIPT LIST

Add. MS 11695. *Silos Apocalypse.* Silos, Spain, c.1073–1109.

Add. MS 15268. *Histoire Universelle.* Latin Kingdom of Jerusalem (Acre), c.1286.

Add. MS 19352. Theodore Psalter. Constantinople, Studios Monastery, 1066.

Add. MS 19587. Dante Alighieri, *The Divine Comedy.* Italy (Naples), c.1370.

Add. MS 23145. Book of Hours. France, c.1370–90.

Add. MS 24686. Alphonso Psalter. England, c.1284.

Add. MS 28681. Psalter. England, c.1262.

Add. MS 36684. Book of Hours. N. France (St Omer), 1340s.

Add. MS 42130. Luttrell Psalter. England, c.1325–1335.

Add. MS 47682. Holkham Bible Picture Book. England, c.1320–1330.

Add. MS 48985. Salvin Hours. England, c.1270.

Add. MS 49622. Gorleston Psalter. England (Gorleston, Suffolk), c.1310–1335.

Add. MS 50,000. Oscott Psalter. Enlgand (Oxford?), c.1265–1270.

Add. MS 54180. *La Somme le Roy.* France (Paris), 1290s.

Add. MS 62925. Rutland Psalter. England (London?), c.1260.

Cotton MS Claudius E V. *Corpus Canonum.* England (Christ Church, Canterbury), c.1120–1130.

Cotton MS Nero C IV. Winchester Psalter. England (Winchester), 1220s.

Cotton MS Tiberius B V. *Wonders of the East* and other texts. England (Winchester?), c.1025–1050.

Cotton MS Tiberius C VI. Tiberius Psalter. England (Winchester), c.1050.

Cotton MS Vitellius A XV. The Beowulf Manuscript, including the *Wonders of the East.* England, c.1000.

Egerton MS 3277. Bohun Psalter. England, probably between 1361–1373.

Harley MS 2506. Pseudo–Bede, *De Cignis Celi.* France (Fleury), late 10th century.

Harley MS 2799. Arnstein Bible. Germany (Arnstein), c.1175.

Harley MS 3244. Bestiary. England, c.1255–1265.

Harley MS 3954. Sir John Mandeville, *Travels.* England, c.1430.

Harley MS 4381. Guyart des Moulins, *La Bible Historiale.* France, c.1403–1404.

Harley MS 4751. Bestiary. England (Salisbury?), c.1230–1240.

Harley MS 4979. Old French Prose Alexander. N. France or S. Netherlands, c.1290–1310.

Royal MS 1 D 1. Bible of William of Devon. Copied by William of Devon. England (Oxford?), c.1260–1270.

Royal MS 2 B VII. Queen Mary Psalter. England (London?), c.1310–1320.

Royal MS 10 E IV. Smithfield Decretals. Copied on the continent and illuminated in England (London), c.1340.

Royal MS 12 F XIII. Bestiary and Lapidary. England (Rochester), c.1220–1240.

Royal MS 15 B VII. Horace, *Ars Poetica.* Germany, c.1175–1200.

Royal MS 15 E VI. Talbot Shrewsbury Book of Romances. France (Rouen), c.1445.

Royal MS 19 B XV. Apocalypse. England, c.1310–1325.

Royal MS 20 A V. Old French Prose Alexander. N. France or Flanders, c.1300–1310.

Stowe MS 17. Book of Hours. Flanders (Liège), c.1300.

Stowe MS 49. Jacobus Voragine, *The Golden Legend (Legenda Aurea)* England, c.1300.

Sloane MS 278. Hugonis de Folleio Aviarium, *Libellus de Naturis Animalium.* France or Flanders, c.1280–1300.

Yates Thompson MS 8. Breviary of Renaud de Bar, Bishop of Metz. France (Verdun?), c.1302.

Yates Thompson MS 10. Apocalypse. France, 1380s.

Yates Thompson MS 13. Taymouth Hours. England (London?), c.1325–1335.

Yates Thompson MS 29. Hours of Bonaparte Ghislieri. Italy (Bologna), c.1500.

INDEX

Alexander the Great 16, 18
Apocalypse 27–28
Aristotle 7

Babewyns 43
Beast, seven headed 28
Bestiary 21–27
Bible 11–12, 27–32, 36, 55
Blemmyae 8, 21, 51
Bottoms 36, 45, 53

Cannibals 21
Centaur 25
Cetus 34
Chimera 43
Christ 12, 15, 22, 36, 38
Ctesias 7
Cyclopes 18
Cynocephali 8, 12

Dante Alighieri, *Divine Comedy* 38
Demons 36, 40, 56
Devil 27, 28, 32, 36, 38, 40
Dragons 8, 15, 18, 23, 28, 32, 34, 50, 58

Giants 8
Griffins 7, 8, 18
Grotesques 43, 44, 45, 50, 53
Gryllus 43

Hell 22, 38, 40
Herodotus 7
Homer 7
Horace 40, 41

Hybrids 41, 43, 47, 50, 53
Hydrus 22

Locusts 27–28

Mandeville, Sir John, *Travels* 5, 21
Mappa Mundi 15
Mermaids 25
Monkeys 53
Monoceros 24
Monstrous races 7, 12, 15

Panotii 10, 51
Pliny the Elder, *Natural History* 7, 21

Satan, see Devil
Sea monsters 34, 58
Serpent 27, 32
Sciopod 5, 51
Siren 25
Solinus 7
Sphinx 19
St Augustine of Hippo 10
St Bernard of Clairvaux 42–3
St George 34
St Margaret 34
St Michael 32

Unicorns 23–24
Universal History 19, 21

Virgin Mary 34, 40

Wild man 55
Wonders of the East 8, 9, 21, 51

63

For Jeremy

THE AUTHOR

Alixe Bovey is a curator in the Department of Manuscripts at The British Library. She received her doctorate from the Courtauld Institute of Art and is currently writing a book about the Smithfield Decretals

Front Cover Illustration:	detail of *Additional MS 62925*, f.57r
Half-title Page:	detail of *Harley MS 4751*, f.62v
Frontispiece:	*Additional MS 54180*, f.14v
Title Page:	detail of *Cotton MS Tiberius B V*, f.82r
Illustration page 4:	*Cotton MS Nero C IV*, f.39r
Back cover:	Scene from the romances of Alexander *Royal MS 15 E VI*, ff.15v–16r

Published in North America in 2002 by
University of Toronto Press Incorporated,
Toronto and Buffalo

National Library of Canada
Cataloguing in Publication Data
Bovey, Alixe
    Monsters and grotesques in
    medieval manuscripts/Alixe Bovey

Co-published by The British Library.
Includes bibliographical references and index

ISBN 0-8020-8512-1

    1. Monsters in art. 2. Grotesques in art. 3. Illumination of books and manuscripts, Medieval.
    4. Christian art and symbolism–Medieval, 500-1500–Themes, motives. I. Title

ND3339.B68 2002   704.9'47   C2002-901889-7

Text © 2002 Alixe Bovey
Illustrations © 2002 The British Library Board
First published 2002 by
The British Library
96 Euston Road
London NW1 2DB

Designed and typeset by Crayon Design, Stoke Row, Henley-on-Thames
Colour origination by Crayon Design and South Sea International Press
Printed in Hong Kong by South Sea International Press